COPING WITH DISCOURAGEMENT

Mary M. Fenocketti

One Liguori Drive
Liguori, Missouri 63057
(314) 464-2500

Dedication

To my friends
S. Beauregard
M. Borkowski
V. Covino

Imprimi Potest:
John F. Dowd, C.SS.R.
Provincial, St. Louis Province
Redemptorist Fathers

Imprimatur:
+ Edward J. O'Donnell
Vicar General, Archdiocese of St. Louis

ISBN 0-89243-226-8

Cover photo by Iner Ford

Copyright © 1985, Liguori Publications

All rights reserved. No part of this booklet may be reproduced, stored in a retrieval system, or transmitted without the written permission of Liguori Publications.

Scripture texts used in this work are taken from the NEW AMERICAN BIBLE, copyright © 1970 by the Confraternity of Christian Doctrine, Washington, D.C., and are used by permission of copyright owner. All rights reserved.

TABLE OF CONTENTS

ONE DAY AT A TIME

DAY 1 5

DAY 2 7

DAY 3 9

DAY 4 11

DAY 5 13

DAY 6 15

DAY 7 17

DAY 8 19

DAY 9 21

DAY 10 23

DAY 11 25

DAY 12 27

DAY 13 29

DAY 14 31

DAY 15 33

DAY 16	35
DAY 17	37
DAY 18	39
DAY 19	41
DAY 20	43
DAY 21	45
DAY 22	47
DAY 23	49
DAY 24	51
DAY 25	53
DAY 26	55
DAY 27	57
DAY 28	59
DAY 29	61
DAY 30	63

DAY 1

May he enlighten your innermost vision that you may know the great hope to which he has called you, the wealth of his glorious heritage to be distributed among the members of the church, and the immeasurable scope of his power in us who believe.

Ephesians 1:18,19

When we are feeling hurt, depressed, or discouraged, it's hard to believe that there is any way out. We may feel trapped. We may feel that there is no solution to our dilemma. In fact, we may actually begin to believe that we have no control at all over our lives. And so the thought that we can actually do something about our troubles, can actually lift ourselves out of our depression, may not even occur to us.

Our innermost vision demands light; light has to be let into the darkness within us. We are encased in a cocoon, and we need to break a little of the shell. All of this sounds fairly mysterious. It needn't be.

The truth is that when we feel bad, our thinking gets very negative. We tend to see life through gray, smoky glasses. Our sad feelings affect how we think — about ourselves, about others, about life in general, and even about God.

Consider this. A package is delivered to your home. There is no return address and the label is typed. There is no way of knowing from whom the package comes or what it contains without opening it. Shaking the box gives no clue. The box is neither very heavy nor very light.

How do you feel about receiving such a package? If your birthday is coming up, you may suspect that this is a gift from someone dear to you (who types labels without giving a return address). On the other hand, if you have received similar packages recently with samples of various items you didn't need, you may be very annoyed.

Life is an unopened package whose contents we do not know ahead of time. The way we react to life depends on what we're thinking and how we're feeling. If we are feeling "down" because we're struggling with a very great problem (the loss of a loved one, the breakup of a relationship, or disappointment at ourselves), then we are not in a very receptive mood.

Hearing that God has great wealth for you and that his power is working in you may be a little hard to swallow at this point. That's OK. Don't force it. It's hard to believe that you are special and to live in secure expectation. But you will — in time.

At this point, since you have made the decision to try to lift yourself up, ask God to open your mind and let in a little of his light. Even if you don't actually see a little hope, even if you are only half-convinced that this will work, ask God and assume that he will answer in his own time. Then, don't wait for beautiful feelings or for the conviction that there is hope. Just go on. Better times will come.

DAY 2

By the might of his glory you will be endowed with the strength needed to stand fast, even to endure joyfully whatever may come.

Colossians 1:11

A promise of strength. Just what we needed! Asking for strength is an admission that we are having a hard time and that we are very lonely trying to shoulder the burden all by ourselves. It is an admission that we need help from Someone who can really support us, Someone powerful and yet understanding.

When we have a defeatist attitude, we cannot use our wonderful human powers. It paralyzes our powers of thinking and acting and puts us out of touch with our feelings. For example, if we have to deal with a person who is, to put it kindly, "difficult," whether critical or stubborn or irritable, we need self-assurance. Only then can we put in perspective the things that are said and done. We can say, "It is his or her problem," and rest assured that whatever the other may do we are still OK.

If we feel bad about ourselves, we tend to side with that other person who is dissatisfied. When we hear our words or motives criticized, we may begin to wonder, "Maybe he is right; maybe I am that way." Then we take the next step — reacting from weakness.

It is always better to act from the strength of self-assurance than from the weakness of diffidence. What's the difference?

We are acting from weakness
— when we accept all of the blame in a two-person situation: when a wife or a husband is willing to shoulder all the responsibility for a troubled marriage and is willing to do all the changing to try to work it out;
— when we let others make important decisions for us, as if we were young children: when we allow our parents to decide whom we should marry, when we should have children;
— when we allow someone to put us down: when we allow our children to talk back to us and simply shrug our shoulders and let it go.

We could go on, but let's concentrate on acting from strength. We all know someone who is a "take-charge" person. This individual enters a messy room and within a short time has everything in order. She knows how to plan, organize, and bring off any kind of event. Such a person is assertive, sure of herself. She does not merely suggest, in a quiet, tentative way. She says "Let's do it this way," hands you the broom, and you find yourself sweeping the floor.

We want to take charge of our lives. We want to act from strength so that we can handle the trials that come. We need to identify the areas where we need strength and to deal with these, one at a time. And we need to remember that God is behind us, silently giving us the strength. When we begin to believe that, yes, we can do it.

DAY 3

For I am certain that neither death nor life, neither angels nor principalities, neither the present nor the future, nor powers, neither height nor depth nor any other creature, will be able to separate us from the love of God that comes to us in Christ Jesus, our Lord.

Romans 8:38-39

One of the problems we should deal with immediately is this: When something bad happens to us, most of us *feel* this means that God does not love us. These feelings are rooted in childhood experience.

When we were children, the withdrawal of tangible love was the worst thing that could happen. We couldn't imagine getting along without parents because we depended so strongly on them. And we judged love through the ways it was expressed — hugs and kisses or special treats, like ice cream cones. When we misbehaved these outward signs were withheld, and the experience was extremely painful.

We are taught that God loves us, as a parent does. We are told that doing good pleases God and that doing what is hurtful does not. As children, many of us got the notion that God didn't love us as much if we were misbehaving as at those times when we were very good.

As mature Christians we should yield such fears to the mature conviction that God loves us, period. His love is not based on our activities, achievements, successes.

Nothing can separate us from the love God has for us; nothing can diminish that love. People can turn their backs on God by a deliberate series of decisions, by a total rejection of God's love. God does not, and never will, turn his back on us.

We may wonder how our problem could possibly be handled. We look at our situation and we are overwhelmed with all kinds of feelings — guilt, anger, sadness. We think, in a very negative way, that there is no hope, that there are no alternatives, that everything is all wrong and always will be.

We are so confused that we wish we could disappear for awhile and come back to find the problem solved. Some of us actually do "drop out" of the situation through drugs, alcohol, and other expressions of despair.

It is absolutely essential to remember that no problem, no matter how great, no matter how much we feel responsible, no matter how personal or how public, can separate us from the real love that God has for us.

If our friends abandon us, if our families reject us, if a spouse turns away, we are not unloved. Even if we cease to love ourselves — even if we give up on ourselves because we just can't stand the pain or the confusion or the exhaustion — even then, God still loves us.

We may not feel loved. We may not think we are loved. We may have convinced ourselves of this, but it is not true. God does love us. Become deeply committed to this conviction by repeating it habitually in prayer.

DAY 4

. . . God keeps his promise. He will not let you be tested beyond your strength. Along with the test he will give you a way out of it so that you may be able to endure it.
1 Corinthians 10:13

"Lord, I'm not strong enough. I can't possibly handle this. You know how weak I am."

Many of God's Chosen People have said this: Moses, prophets like Jeremiah, the disciples of Jesus, many of our contemporary religious leaders — and God gave them the strength to do what they had to do.

A widowed friend looks back, two years after her husband died suddenly, and says, "I got through it. I don't know how, but I got the strength. Somehow, little by little, I did it."

A woman who fought depression, a depression so severe that she literally feared she could not get through the day, marvels that, somehow, the dark tunnel of her despair is now behind her. "There were times when incredible things happened. There was one morning that was particularly bad, when I just didn't think I would make it. The phone rang at a quarter to eight; a friend who seldom called was on the line. Her friendly call got me through the morning. I realized that Someone was watching over me."

When we're feeling bad, reminding ourselves that God keeps his promises may not seem to "take." When we are feeling low, we think low. "This is one promise God won't keep. Not in my case. I mean, there's no way out. What if I fail and just give up and what if. . . . "

At times we cannot see a way out. We really can't. It's like driving in a fog on a strange road. Our destination may be just yards away, but we can't see it until we're almost there. A solution, too, may be just steps away, but we cannot see it. Our life is too muddled. Sometimes we just have to wait a bit until it is clear. Sometimes we have to push through the fog a little.

God never allows us to reach the point where we cannot get through it; however, we must remember that God's notion of success and ours may differ. Sometimes the solution is painful and difficult. Sometimes it involves taking steps that we have never taken before — steps we may never have even imagined. For example, we may need to end a painful relationship, leave a job, have surgery, enter a rehabilitation program.

Sometimes we have no idea where to turn and no idea what to do. Let's remind the Lord of his promise to help us in times of testing; let's ask the Lord what to do.

Praying may be difficult. We need only do the very basic thing — ask for help — and wait. Hard as that may seem, we must wait.

DAY 5

May he who is the Lord of peace give you continued peace in every possible way. The Lord be with you all.
2 Thessalonians 3:16

We can deal with even the most difficult problems when we are at peace. Anxiety hampers our efforts, and it is prevalent.

Contemporary psychologists speak of "the anxiety attack," a very painful phenomenon. People who experience it, and you may have, find themselves so overwhelmed with fear when faced with stressful situations that they have to leave the scene. The physiological symptoms are varied, but their emotional roots are apparent. The treatment is complex because anxiety is complex.

"Peace, peace, and there is no peace." Peace is hard to attain, even if our lives are fairly smooth. The very fact that we are members of families, that we are hardworking adults, that we have to earn a living, that we are responsible for our children, that we have to juggle many responsibilities, means that our peace will be hard come by.

Peace demands a turning away from all too natural anxiety and a journey in search of a healthy state of mind. We start by trying to work out the difficulties we face, and work toward something we see as a source of happiness.

When we are feeling sad or troubled we are not at peace. We become overwhelmed with a feeling of powerlessness; our troubles control us. We feel like a little lost puppy, with no source of comfort. Only when we attain some sense of control do we begin to relax and find peace.

How do we control situations which seem out of control — a marriage which is crumbling, a chronic illness that is "just too much," the serious sickness of a spouse, the problems of sons or daughters, turmoil in the family, sadness or loneliness?

First, we need to stop trying to do everything alone. We have an obligation as members of the human community to share what we have with others, and that includes what is hurting us. We must reach out to others, to our family and friends, to professional helpers. After all, why do we insist on fighting alone? Isn't it for fear that no one will understand, that people will think less of us, that we will appear weak or afraid. Of course, we take that risk when we share our burdens with others; but we blow it out of all proportion. There are also some situations which warrant professional help. We should be realistic in our expectations and honest with ourselves.

The first step, then, is to let go of the need to fight alone — we have to let go. We need to share — with the people around us and with the Lord who, unlike the others, understands perfectly. We can even ask him to take the burden for awhile so that we can rest.

You can begin to find peace when you seek it, when you ask for it, and when you keep on asking.

DAY 6

... we have been praying for you unceasingly and asking that you may attain full knowledge of his will through perfect wisdom and spiritual insight. Then you will lead a life worthy of the Lord and pleasing to him in every way. You will multiply good works of every sort and grow in the knowledge of God.

Colossians 1:9,10

What does God want *for* us? What should we be doing? How should we go about attacking our problems? How can we keep on going and work out of our discouragement?

Knowing what God's will means is a lifelong search. It is not a black and white matter, choosing the obvious good over the obvious bad thing. Life is full of grays, full of choices. Each day, because we are human and free, we make hundreds of choices. How do we know how to decide? Does it matter?

Friends taught me to start each day with a prayer that goes like this: "Lord, take me where you want me to go. Lead me where you want me to be." It expresses the willingness to be in tune with what God wants. God's will is not something so mysterious that we must fear it. God's will can only lead, step by step, to the Lord who is, after all, the reason for our life.

In answering the question, "Is this God's will?" there are some guidelines:

Is this a loving thing to do?

Am I helping and not hurting?

Does this conform to my own life values?

What would Jesus do?

When we are feeling discouraged, making decisions is particularly difficult and dangerous. Psychiatrists recommend that we put off major decisions at such times until we are stronger and are thinking more clearly.

One important decision, however, cannot be delayed — the decision to attack our problem intelligently, not to be controlled by it. You should be happy that you have come to that point: You know you have a problem and that you can't let things remain as they are. An alcoholic who says, "I do have a problem; I need help," is on the way to a solution. So are the depressed who seek professional help; the chronically ill who decide it's not enough to just bear the pain; mothers who decide that they will no longer be overwhelmed by their obligations; and the men who admit that their jobs are costing too much in terms of health and stress and have decided to seek other work.

Little decisions can become difficult, too. We are faced with so many, no matter how we feel. But we need to realize that no decision can actually ruin our lives; no decision is absolute; every decision may later involve minor regrets.

Ask God for the beginning of this kind of wisdom — to better know his will and to desire to do it.

DAY 7

If God is for us, who can be against us?

Romans 8:31

God loves us. God cares about us. God is behind us through thick and thin, through the dark nights and the long days, through the joys and the sorrows, always. God is on our side. So why are we so unhappy?

Another need that many of us carry over from childhood is the need for approval by authority figures. It was appropriate in childhood. If we did what our parents told us, whether that was making our beds or putting away our toys, we enjoyed their approval. If we didn't, we suffered their disapproval.

As adults, many of us continue to act in the same way; we are just as sensitive to what those think who are important to us. We continually look over our shoulders and consider what they are thinking about us.

For example, we want to speak up when someone slights us, but we hesitate because we are afraid of what they may think. We fail to deal with the question of where to spend the holidays because we are afraid of what the family will think.

Some of us have been carrying around for years the hurts inflicted by others who may not even be aware that they offended us. And we never say anything, we never even admit to ourselves what we are suffering — because of what "they" may think.

Many of our problems with saying "Yes" when we want to say "No," or saying "No" when we want to say "Yes," stem from fear of what the other person will think. I know people who are tremendously overextended because they are afraid to refuse for fear of appearing selfish.

What if the thing we fear most — disapproval — is there? We do affect others; we do need their support. It hurts when we do not have it. It really hurts.

But the fact is that disapproval is not the worst thing in the world. Disappointing ourselves is a far greater hurt; we cannot hide from ourselves. And even if the dearest one in the world does not approve, it is not hopeless. I know several women who are still struggling with the problem of getting along with their mothers, though the daughters are well into their forties and fifties. Though married, they still seek mother's approval; they do not have it and they feel inadequate, not because they do anything wrong but just because they are themselves.

If God is for us, and God *always* is, if we are honestly seeking to please him and God is so important, then whose disapproval can hurt us?

DAY 8

. . . we boast of our hope for the glory of God. But not only that — we even boast of our afflictions! We know that affliction makes for endurance, and endurance for tested virtue, and tested virtue for hope.

Romans 5:2-4

The first time I heard the expression "Adversity builds character," I really bristled. Really! Who cares about character when you feel so discouraged you want to cry. And how could it possibly be helpful to remind someone who is having a hard time of it of the benefits to "character."

But think about this: After you've muddled through troubles and come out OK, don't you feel that you may have gained something from the experience? Not at first, when you're still worn out and tired, but after a while.

A friend went through a very difficult period of ill health, seeking medical treatment for her ailments, being told more than once that it was "all in her head," and suffering the effects of medicine that wasn't correct. Finally, after years of searching, her condition was correctly diagnosed and appropriate treatment started. It's hard to see how she got anything from all this, but she insists she has. And she is confident that as the years go by she will become stronger and stronger, though her illness will never leave her.

You are going through a hard time now, and you want very much to be finished with it. With the help of God, yourself, and your friends, you should be able to fight and be strong. But the thought that this may actually be a growing period may be repugnant at this point. Again, negative thinking comes in. This hurts; it can't possibly be good; I can't see a solution; I'm never going to understand.

Remember, now is not the time to judge whether your trial will produce something of value. Only distance will enable you to make that assessment. But it may help to consider what others have found — that they do come through difficulties stronger than ever.

When we think of endurance, we may think of the long-distance runner. Being a marathon runner has acquired status in contemporary society. It certainly must be exciting to achieve this. But we all know that to run a marathon we have to go into training, we have to start slowly, we have to get in condition. When the final race is run, it is the culmination of a long period of practice and hard work. During that race, the runner draws on the strength he or she has built up through daily discipline and practice. Without the agony and the pain of training, this race is not feasible.

When we are running in our own life's marathon, let's remember that the hard times give us strength. Just how much is hard to see now; at the end of the race it will be clear.

DAY 9

We are afflicted in every way possible, but we are not crushed; full of doubts, we never despair. We are persecuted but never abandoned; we are struck down but never destroyed.

2 Corinthians 4:8-9

Saint Paul had suffered extreme hardships: imprisonment, beatings, humiliations, conflict at every turn. Others might have been destroyed by such circumstances, but not Paul.

Paul had seen the first martyr, Stephen, empowered to pray for those who stoned him (while Paul held their cloaks!). Paul had been knocked off his horse by the source of Stephen's great power. And Paul had come to accept that same powerful Person into his life as his "friend" and the source of a love stronger than pain, suffering, or death.

When we feel discouraged, we do not feel like fighting. We shy away from actually rolling up our sleeves and attacking our problems. It is so much less painful to retreat.

There are people — perhaps you are among them — who feel that they are crushed, that there is no hope, and that they truly do not have a friend. They may even feel that they have been destroyed. For each of us, there is a limit to our tolerance of pain, not just physical pain but psychic pain. There is only so much we can bear, and then we cannot bear any more.

What can you do? What can you do to fight this, to keep on hoping when each step is so painful? Start by remembering:

No matter how hopeless everything may seem, things "bottom out" and then get better.
Every depression that is dealt with eventually lifts.
There were times in your life when you were happy; you will feel this way again.

Pray for a fighting spirit, for a love of life. I always thought of my paternal grandfather as a kind of Santa Claus. He had snowy white hair and blue eyes that twinkled. He had a difficult life, as most immigrants of the turn of the century had, working on the railroad, trying to raise a large family. What I remember most clearly about him is the celebration of his 75th birthday. He insisted on the full number of candles. We all sang, all of his sons and daughters and grandchildren, and then, with a smile, he blew out all 75 candles with one massive breath, filling the crowded kitchen with smoke. Then the men sang Italian songs, and I shivered with pleasure as I still do when I remember that day. That man had what the philosophers call *joie de vivre*, the joy of living, love of life.

When you feel bad, pray for the basic gut-level momentum to live each moment fully, joyfully, vigorously. When we're discouraged this is so hard, but what wish could be more worthwhile? With joy, we can really live our lives, be ourselves, and give to others.

DAY 10

As we have shared much in the suffering of Christ, so through Christ do we share abundantly in his consolation.
2 Corinthians 1:5

When we think about the sufferings of Christ, our attention is first drawn to his crucifixion and death; and these, while moving, seem far removed from the kind of suffering we experience. We may make the mistake of believing that our suffering is insignificant by comparison. But whatever we suffer is a sharing in his suffering.

Suffering, of course, means nothing in itself. It is not a good thing, and it gains us nothing unless we suffer for a purpose. Individuals who use their suffering as a base for reaching out to others, as do recovering alcoholics who give their time counseling others, make their suffering meaningful. The person paralyzed with a stroke makes that sense of helplessness meaningful by using the time to build up strength and spiritual power.

Jesus suffered many of the same things that we suffer; his "in-tuneness" with the Father elevated them to the point of meaningfulness. As a boy in the Temple, he suffered the loneliness that comes from others not understanding our needs. He later suffered rejection by his own townspeople, the people with whom he had grown up. He was completely misunderstood by his friends who still awaited an earthly kingdom, though he had always taught them otherwise. He suffered physical pain, spiritual desolation, in the agony in the garden. When we today suffer these things — misunderstanding, rejection, humiliation — we can unite ourselves to Christ and ask for strength through him.

There are ways we suffer that Christ never knew; when we endure these, we complete what he suffered. Jesus never suffered the trial of cancer or the chronic pain of arthritis or such stress-related illnesses as hypertension, ulcers, migraine headaches. Jesus never suffered the pain of an unhappy marriage, of a child who runs away, or of a parent who is ungrateful.

Still, there is no reason to feel alone; because we have the same source of support that he had. What was it that kept Jesus going? The conviction that he had a mission from his Father and his constant "in-tuneness" with the Father. He prayed — in fact, he spent days in prayer. When he asked that the suffering be taken away, in the garden, he gained strength and help, though he still suffered. He was never without Someone to help.

This is not to say that Jesus escaped that sense of feeling abandoned that sometimes comes to people who are discouraged. His cry, "My God, why have you abandoned me?" shows us something: that help can be very close, yet we may feel lost and alone. Jesus knew discouragement, as you do. And he felt the need for a helping hand, though that seemed not to be near. But he did always receive consolation, and that same kind of support is there for us.

DAY 11

God is not unjust; he will not forget your work and the love you have shown him by your service, past and present, to his holy people.

Hebrews 6:10

God is not unfair. But sometimes life is. This is one of the most difficult facts to face.

We develop certain assumptions, in childhood, about how life is going to be. If I am good, I will be rewarded; if I do something bad, I will suffer. Whatever we experience will even out in the end. Our sense of justice as children is strong — we need to believe that everything is fair and square. We grow up thinking this way: If I study, I will pass; if I graduate with honors, I'll find a great job; if I work hard, I'll be happy; if I'm married, I'll never be lonely.

Then, at some point, the realization dawns on us that life is not fair. We may see how much someone we love suffers, and we just know they don't deserve it. When a friend lost her husband it really wasn't fair. She had been through so much herself — a battle with alcohol that she overcame and is still overcoming. The prolonged critical illness of a baby. Widowed, she has to support two teenagers on a job that is less than satisfying. Yet, there are others, with those healthy kids, that loving husband, and excellent job; not a perfect life but, obviously, not as full of heavy burdens.

I have known several people so afflicted with arthritis that each step was excruciating. Their lives were saturated with pain. Other people never seem to endure physical pain; they do have trials, but they do not know the burden of the arthritic person.

God is not unjust. He knows what you do. He loves you. While others forget or disregard what you do for them, he never forgets. "Nobody notices what I do," laments the homemaker. No one thanks her for the meals lovingly prepared, the clean house, the gift of time and energy she continually gives. God does not forget.

Often, being unappreciated seems to come with our territory. Self-centeredness is prevalent: a great deal of concentrating on what *I* need, on what *you* need. It's often chalked up to the hectic pace with which we live out our lives. But that's no excuse. We ought to express our appreciation and thanks, and affirm those who care for us. If we did, we would all feel that wonderful sense of being loved and wanted. But we don't.

So many people say, "I feel drained. I give and give, and I have nothing more to give." It's true. It is possible to feel so unappreciated that we become like a tired old sponge — dried out. But, though it's natural to want to count in the eyes of others, we must never become totally dependent upon human appreciation.

We have to be convinced that God is not unjust. He will even out the score at the end of the game, in the forever.

DAY 12

Dismiss all anxiety from your minds. Present your needs to God in every form of prayer and in petitions full of gratitude.

Philippians 4:6

"Worry is like a rocking chair," someone told me. "It gets you nowhere." It's so true, but how many of us feel incomplete if we are not actively worrying about something.

You have a problem which is troubling you. How can you possibly avoid anxiety? While a certain amount of concern is inevitable, how can you avoid making yourself more upset by needless worrying? Ask yourself these questions:

Did I ever solve a problem by worrying about it?
Did I ever worry a great deal and then find that what I feared most did not happen?
Do I feel funny not worrying?
Do I worry about all kinds of things?
Does worrying make me feel more in control?

If you are discouraged, begin by breaking the problem into manageable pieces. For example, if you must deal with a spouse troubled by alcoholism, try not to concentrate on the total picture too much. If you have decided to confront your spouse and insist on his or her seeking help, do not worry about the long-term repercussions. Make the decision and deliberately avoid worrying. Tell yourself that worrying will not help. Once the confrontation has taken place, do not spend any energy worrying about whether the other will seek help. Simply refuse to worry; this takes hard work, but with persistence you will succeed.

When we feel particularly discouraged, we worry more. We don't have the confidence to see that everything will come out all right; but we can, little by little, learn to rely on Someone more powerful.

Instead of worrying, get into the habit of leaving the problem in God's hands. The expression "Let go and let God" has become very popular. We all admit it's sound advice, but practicing it is not so simple.

"Let go of your problem." "Work as if everything depended on you, and pray as if everything depended on God." Do what you can, and then hand it over to the one who really can relieve you of the burden.

"Let God" — allow God to work on the problem. And give God time. Does it make sense to expect a quick solution to a complex problem? We hand God a problem which has taken us years and years to develop, and we expect an answer right away. If we don't get it that fast, we take it back and try to solve it by ourselves, though we failed in the past.

When we ask God to take over, let's do so expecting the best. We talk about faith that can move mountains, but we are hesitant to take leaps of faith and really ask God to keep his promises. We all remember so many wonderful things that God has done in our lives; let's ask him to do the same now — when we are especially needy.

DAY 13

There is cause for rejoicing here. You may for a time have to suffer the distress of many trials.

1 Peter 1:6

No one wants to be sad. You'd be surprised at how many people believe that if a person is sad or distressed it is because they are giving in, that they are not trying hard enough to be happy, that they really somehow "enjoy" feeling bad.

Any depressed person will tell you that this is simply not true. When you feel sad, you'd give anything to feel better, to get rid of the thoughts and feelings that pull you down. You are reading this precisely because you want to feel better; you want to get over all that brings you down.

Sometimes it is necessary to be sad, to pass through a time of distress in order to grow. This is true whenever we mourn. After someone close to us dies we have a period of mourning to go through, and we must work through that in order to go on with our lives. We need to take the time. We need to accept the sadness, not because we enjoy it, but because it is part of the process of saying farewell to the dear one and, then, picking up the pieces and continuing our own journey.

At times, we are in mourning for ourselves. We go through struggles; we fail at times; our past and our present and our future frighten or disappoint us. It's OK to be sad, as long as we don't lose perspective.

People with chronic illness may mourn at the signs of weakness or aging because they sense that they are dying a little at a time. Facing and accepting and understanding this enables them to get through this difficult period and to get back to living their lives as fully as possible.

At times the problems with which we struggle seem to overwhelm us, and we are sad. This sadness can become a source of growth. But severe or prolonged sadness is a sign that we need to seek help from professionals. There is no reason to be embarrassed about responding to the very real need to be healed.

Still you can't yield to moodiness without fighting. If you wake up one morning and just don't feel like getting out of bed, of course you may decide to do just that — stay in bed all day. But your mood won't improve. If, on the other hand, you try very, very hard to get up and around, you will certainly be taking important steps in the direction of dissolving your sad state. You might, for example, take an early morning walk, go to a church service, or call a friend and make an appointment for lunch.

When you are sad it helps a great deal to feel that you can accomplish something, however small. When you do, your bad feelings will be at least partially neutralized by your sense of accomplishment. Try to find some small task which you can do, and see if you don't feel better for having made the effort. In this way, though you must go through a time of sadness, you yourself can take away some of the pain.

DAY 14

My prayer is that your love may more and more abound, both in understanding and wealth of experience, so that with a clear conscience and blameless conduct you may learn to value the things that really matter. . . .
Philippians 1:9,10

How do we know what is best? As we said earlier, making important decisions is usually to be avoided when we feel discouraged. But sometimes indecision is the cause of our sadness. Perhaps we have endured an intolerable situation for too long but have been unable to act. How can we make the effort?

Infinite love, complete understanding, and broad experience are, of course, ideal. We simply do not possess them. We do our best. When we make a decision, we do the best we can under the circumstances. We can be very logical, list the pros and cons, discover what could have the better results, and still may not want to make the choice that is called for. We may feel very strongly that there is only one solution, but when we contemplate it we may find it too painful. In our discouragement we may be thinking negatively, and all alternatives may appear equally poor.

Perhaps we need to step back a little from our situation in order to come to a satisfactory conclusion. It might help to ask ourselves, "If our best friend had this problem, what would we advise her to do?"

We should definitely not go it alone. We should enlist the help of others — the help of the right people — of those who are able to understand the situation and to be honest and intelligent. Of course, we are never bound to accept the advice of others. In fact, we should never make an important decision on the basis of what someone else insists is the only option. To do so would be to not make the decision ourselves, and we would probably resent it later. For example, a mature person who breaks off an engagement to be married solely because of family disapproval will certainly be bitter.

Occasionally, our sadness comes from a decision which we made long ago and which we regret deeply. If you were the driver of a car involved in an automobile accident in which people were injured, you may be tempted to relive the situation over and over, wondering why you went this way instead of that, why you slammed on the brakes instead of pumping them, or why you swerved this way. The trouble with this kind of analysis is that it is made now — when you have both the knowledge of the outcome (the accident) and the leisure to consider very carefully how you might have acted if given more time. In emergency situations, we react the best we can at the time, given our instant assessment of the situation. We always act to avoid an accident, so we should not be too hard on ourselves. If there is blame, we should accept that; if there is none, we should not create it.

The bottom line is that we cannot redo the past. We are left to deal with the consequences of our decisions. This does not mean that we are doomed to misery because of one faulty decision. As we grow in love and understanding and experience, our decisions will be easier but never without effort or occasional regrets.

DAY 15

. . . he . . . set me apart before I was born and called me by his favor.

Galatians 1:15

God set you apart before you were born — in his wisdom and in his love. Somehow, it's not so hard to believe that God had such a great love that he was willing to share life with us. The idea that God in his *wisdom* called us, however, is harder to see. But God has chosen to depend on us to do his work in the world. So he has a calling for you; he needs you to do something special for him and for your brothers and sisters in the human community. But even beyond this, God needs *you*. No one can take your place. You are unique. There is only one you. Try to see it this way — if you were not here, who would be there? Perhaps someone else, but not you.

If God chose you, why are you unhappy? Perhaps you feel that you have failed in one or more of the important areas in your life. You may feel that you are to blame, that you are not worthwhile, that you are "just no good." But, you see, God chose you, knowing that you would not be perfect, that you would have to struggle, that you would sometimes not measure up to the best in you. God called you anyway.

We used to talk as though only certain people had a calling; those called to the priestly or community religious life. Most of us remember the picture of the young girl with the angel in her shadow and the caption, "Is God calling me?" Yes, he was calling her, and he is calling you and me. He chose us before we ever were, and continues to call us to meet the challenges that life brings.

God calls us to serve him. But how can we serve him when we feel bad? God knows human nature fully; he knows our ups and downs and that we tend to think that we can only work well when we feel in top shape. Physical, emotional, spiritual problems get in our *way*.

Some of us are too hard on ourselves. We have a tendency to look at only the outcome of our efforts and to judge them harshly. We have a "report card" kind of mentality. We grade ourselves constantly: "I spoke too soon." "I said too much." "I should have cleaned that." "That turned out poorly."

If we must grade ourselves, let's be entirely fair. We really should stop measuring only the outcome and should start recognizing EFFORT. We tell our children that as long as they try hard we will be satisfied with their schoolwork. If we are really trying hard, then there is no reason to call ourselves failures.

Perhaps there are areas in our life that need attention. Then, by all means, give them that attention. But let's remember that God chose us because of, not in spite of, who we are.

DAY 16

. . . the mystery of Christ in you, your hope of glory. This is the Christ we proclaim while we admonish all men.

Colossians 1:27,28

Why is Christ in you? In you, the singular "you," distinct from anyone else? Do you feel he made a mistake and should have chosen somewhere else to dwell?

Christ is in you because you are a fitting vessel, because you need him, and because he needs you to present him to the world. Most of the time we tend to forget that Christ is in us, and this may be one reason that we're so dissatisfied with ourselves.

Even if we have been aware of Christ's presence, times of trouble force us to reexamine our lives. Sadness may obscure the reality of Christ's presence. It's like being out at night — we need to be reassured that what was there in the daytime is there now. We need to take our spiritual flashlight and look in the corners, into the dark places.

Most of us were brought up to avoid having company in our home if it was not clean and tidied up. We don't answer the door if we're not properly dressed. We would be embarrassed to have a friend overhear a family argument. All normal fears. But we needn't have the same fears with Christ. He is truly "one of us." He wants us to "come as we are."

It's important to know this because it means that we don't have to be in our best mood or in a very happy state to communicate with our Lord. We don't have to be feeling good;

our thoughts may be muddled. We needn't worry. In our darkest hour, we can "open up" to the Lord in us.

Learning to see Christ in others is a beautiful habit. It's easy to see Christ in:

> the baby, dressed in white and lace on her baptismal day;
> the child, radiant after receiving First Holy Communion;
> the husband who remembers your birthday;
> the wife who cooks a roast to perfection;
> the parents who always seem to understand;
> the child who brings you a bunch of dandelions.

It's harder to be aware of Christ in:

> the kid who's always grimy and noisy;
> the spouse who is battling alcoholism;
> the adolescent who slams his door and shouts, "You don't want me around!"
> the parent who is demanding or complaining.

At times, it's hardest of all to see Christ IN YOU. This may be true even though the good you do makes others aware of the Christ who continues his life of love in you. It's good to reflect on this, too, at those awful times.

DAY 17

You must know that your body is a temple of the Holy Spirit, who is within — the Spirit you have received from God.
1 Corinthians 6:19

Because the Lord dwells in us, we need to take care of ourselves. We need to become aware of just how precious, unique, and necessary we are.

We must remind ourselves that we are still a temple:

when we are physically ill, and in pain;
when we are weak, aged, paralyzed by a stroke, bedridden;
when we are troubled, afraid, or lonely;
when we are either dying — or mourning;
when we are despairing, without faith and feeling unloved.

The problem often arises because we are not convinced that other people see us as precious. They criticize, hurt, neglect us — and we are tempted to think that perhaps we do not deserve kindness and respect.

Mothers sometimes get the feeling that they are just there to pick up after the other (more important?) people in the family, because no one seems to appreciate them. People who work in monotonous jobs may think it doesn't matter whether they go to work or not — that someone else would do the job if they were gone, and no one would miss them. Teachers tend to doubt their impact; adolescents weary of being misunderstood. Grandfathers wonder whether anyone remembers; and elderly ladies whether there is still love in the world.

While it would be wonderful if everyone did appreciate us, we can't sit back and wait for that. We have to try to help ourselves. We have to learn to build up our own confidence. We have to get over making our lives out as impossible, or we'll never get on top of things.

Reminding ourselves that we are temples means that we must take care of ourselves. If we are ill, we must seek and follow the treatment. If we are troubled, we must look for help. If we are sad, we must learn to deal with it. If we feel that others take advantage of us, we must become sensitively assertive. Certainly, we must not hurt others in the process of improving our situation; but we must be just to ourselves as well as to others.

Starting to live with the awareness of our being temples means that we have to deal with those others who don't treat us with that respect. We must take the initiative. Mothers must enlist the help of the family so that their burdens do not become too heavy. Elderly persons must approach others and be sure that they themselves are approachable. Teachers should stretch their vision beyond the current semester. Assembly line workers must focus with pride on the "cars" they are building rather than the bolts they are tightening.

Taking pride in being what we are, temples of God, does not mean that we will boast or act superior. But the confidence that comes from knowing who we are and who is within us gives us strength and enables us to better perform the work to which God calls us.

DAY 18

. . . Does something molded say to its molder, "Why did you make me like this?"

Romans 9:20

So many times we look around and wonder, "Why am I the way I am? Why am I so quiet, so impatient, so plain — so dull?" And we don't stop there. We keep going: "Why am I not more beautiful, more loving, more prayerful — more like that other person over there?" We compare, and we always come up short.

It takes many of us a lifetime to stop fighting who we are, to stop complaining that we are this way when we want to be that way, to stop regretting what we do, and to stop wishing for what we don't have. When a popular singer tells you "I've got to be me," you agree and feel that it must be easy for him. But do you have the conviction, deep inside you, that you have really got to be yourself, not someone else, not what you feel "others" expect you to be?

Certainly self-improvement is good, and we'd all stop growing without it. We owe it to ourselves and our happiness to work on our rough edges, to round out the sharp corners of our personality. But the person we're working on will be, deep-down, the one we are now. We are not really going to be able to make ourselves over; and yet, so many of us try to do just that.

We try to be the person who has everything we do not, an enthusiastic, never grouchy, never tired, never sad, even-tempered, nonexistent, completely "other" person. Sometimes we do this on our own. We just aren't satisfied with what we are. But we go too far. We want to throw out the old person and start from scratch. That can't be done. Beneath the most expert job at renovation is the same structure, the same person, that same clay pot that God fashioned.

More often, we try to redo ourselves in response to what we feel others expect of us. To a certain extent, every child is molded by the image he or she sees in the eyes of his or her parents. In adulthood, many of us are still affected by that image, though our parents are absent. The image has been transferred to the eyes of a spouse or others important to us. While it's good to care about what others want, it is not wise to make ourselves over, hoping for approval. To give the impression that we would do anything, even change into someone else's image, just to be loved reveals a kind of desperation that is unhealthy. It is not real love.

"I like you just the way you are," says Fred Rogers to the children who watch his television show. That message is what we want to hear. If we don't hear it from those around us, we must become aware of God saying it in the fact of our very existence.

God fashioned us — these unique pots of clay that we are. And he was able to make us just the way he wanted us!

DAY 19

Let us, then, be children no longer, tossed here and there, carried about by every wind of doctrine that originates in human trickery and skill in proposing error. Rather, let us profess the truth in love and grow to the full maturity of Christ the head.

Ephesians 4:14-15

Many of us are still children when it comes to faith. We have never gone beyond the kind of religion that eight- or ten-year-olds have, which is certainly incomplete.

We spoke earlier of how many of us retain the notion that God doesn't love us as much when we are misbehaving as at those times when we are doing our best. Many of us also seem to take from childhood the fear that if God does not seem to answer our prayers, if we do not "get" what we want, then God may not be listening.

We need to grow up in Christ. One of the key elements in maturity is coming to grips with the reality of suffering in this life. We are good people, and yet we suffer. This makes no sense to a child, who assumes that if we are good no harm will come to us.

Actually, we may be reinforcing this attitude in our own children. Education aims at preparing the student for a career — the assumption is that if you study hard you will find a job and you will succeed. It doesn't make any sense out of failure. Yet, we know that sometimes adults fail: instead of fulfillment, they find brokenness. We also know that failure can be a bridge to success, as lessons are learned.

If you are still thinking as a child, then you need to try to grow up in Christ. You must learn to be strong. First, take stock.

Just what is important to you?
What areas of your faith life need development?
Are you quick to falter in your faith?
How do you react to suffering? Do you feel guilty?

You know that people who suffer a great deal of physical pain may get to the point where they will try anything — anything at all — just to get relief. Often, they are deceived and become the prey of dishonest "quacks," who offer easy solutions to complicated problems. In our faith life we may be tempted to seek easy solutions to the spiritual dilemmas that confound us — to abandon our faith and to give up on Christ, to try to find something or someone more satisfying.

There are no easy ways of maturing in faith. Maturity involves suffering, painful choices, difficult decisions. It involves trying as though trust didn't count and trusting as though trying didn't count.

DAY 20

. . . Now is the acceptable time! Now is the day of salvation!
2 Corinthians 6:2

Why wait? Begin today to take action. Begin today to actively seek the solutions to your problems, to actively open to God's favor.

Someone suggested to me that we should remind God of his promises; we don't have to. I have a sticker that shows a colorful rainbow encircling the words, "God keeps his promises." What does it mean?

We all know that the rainbow is a sign of something very special — it's a sign of hope in some distant treasure, that pot of gold that is so far away, always just beyond our grasp. We can reach that pot of gold (happiness) by following the rainbow. How do we make that journey?

We need to have dreams. We need to have hopes. We need to want to see a little *beyond* our horizon, to reach a little beyond our means. "Man's grasp is beyond his reach; else what's a heaven for?" In other words, we need to reach a little beyond today, to tomorrow, to forever — to heaven and eternal happiness.

So, we decide to follow the particular rainbow in our life; but where do we start? First, we have to begin to think of ourselves as part of the caravan of humanity. We make a trip, at one and the same time, alone and with others. We make a contribution — a unique contribution — to the dream of humanity while in quest of our own dream.

The amazing thing about this rainbow — and all rainbows — is that you can go very far indeed and still seem to be just as far from the end. This is because the rainbow is with us on the journey; there is joy to be found in the journeying. But at some point, which is unique to each of us, the searching ends; and suddenly in a blaze of light we will realize that we are at the end of the rainbow.

The journey is different for each of us, and we would like to know in advance a little about it. Who are we? Why are we here? But even as we ponder these questions, we cannot stop traveling. We wonder where we are going, but something inside tells us we should go.

Thinking of ourselves in this way makes it easier to be aware of the transitory nature of our lives, with the horizons constantly changing. God has promised us that pot of gold — and we must remind ourselves that this is why we are here.

"Someday we'll find it, the rainbow connection," says the song. But today, we must start looking. Today, let's start believing in it. And let's actively work out of our discouragement by getting on the road and setting our spiritual sights in the right direction.

God is always there, ready to lead us, but we have to look up and around to see him. Look up, look around, but don't look too far. We don't need to.

DAY 21

But if the choice is by grace, it is not because of their works — otherwise grace would not be grace.

Romans 11:6

Do you have the feeling that you never do enough? You're always busy doing what needs to be done, doing for others, for the family, the community; but it's never enough. "The hurrieder I go, the behinder I get." The more we hurry, the more that needs doing.

Sometimes it seems that everything you do is wrong. Everything you do meets with disapproval. You keep hearing critical remarks. And the trouble is that when you feel down your energy level is lower. It's an effort to do even the ordinary things that just have to be done — meal preparation, housekeeping, the office work. And just when you get to the point of saying to yourself "I've done what has to be done and that's enough," they remind you of all that you haven't done. "Mom, when are you going to hem my skirts?" "Dad, you promised to take me to Scouts." "Dear, would you give me a hand with cleaning the attic?" Sometimes they're gentle in their reminders, and sometimes they just don't seem to understand.

You've been feeling bad, and now you feel worse. You don't feel that you are pulling your weight.

Let's stop this. God created us because of his great love. His choice to give us life was not based on something we did first, nor does the fullness of that life demand nonstop activity. We do not have to keep very busy and accomplish a great deal to earn his love.

Yet, we may feel that we should be doing more to repay God's love. If we say so many prayers, if we do so many more good deeds, if we say "I'm sorry" so many different ways, then maybe we'll start to even the score. No, this isn't so. We don't have to scurry around, inventing ways to please God, going out of our way to prove our love. Love expresses itself through ordinary, spontaneous thoughts and actions.

We can show our love for God by simply following our daily routine — it's just that simple, and it's just that complicated. It's not the clean house or the scrubbed kids or the excellently written report or the perfect test paper that does it. It's the *way* we do these things. We can actually do nothing at times, and that too is OK. Yes, it is! Simply relaxing, when there are no tasks that must be attended to at that moment, is perfectly acceptable. We don't need to feel guilty for living an ordinary life with its ups and downs.

We will certainly want to help others and put a great deal of energy into it. But we don't need to develop a list of accomplishments. When we come to the end of our lives we will not be asked for a detailed résumé of all we have done, but quite simply, "Were you loving?"

DAY 22

This means that if anyone is in Christ, he is a new creation. The old order has passed away; now all is new!
2 Corinthians 5:17

There's a lot of talk these days about being "reborn." Those who have experienced it want to talk about it. Their lives seem to have begun again because something special happened — they became acutely aware of the Lord. He was within them all the time, but at some point they took notice.

For most of us, rebirth is a gradual process. Little by little, we come to realize the truth that has always been there — that Christ is in us, our source of hope and joy.

In any case, whether we have a dramatic or a gradual rebirth, we remain the same person throughout. We may say, "I'm a new person," in the sense that so much has changed that we don't feel at all like what we were before. Union with Christ is a profound change; but the person, the "you" in that new relationship, is the same. I think it's important to remember this for several reasons. First, we needn't feel there is something basically wrong with us or that rebirth means throwing out what is unique to us. Second, we want to guard against feeling that rebirth will solve all our problems or that all our faults will disappear.

Let's look at it this way. Rebirth into a life with Christ is possible for all of us. I think we can see it as a change in orientation, a change in direction.

If we are traveling on a ship toward the east, we have a certain orientation: The sun rises in front of us and sets behind us. We have a certain horizon. If the ship changes direction so that it travels toward the west, our orientation becomes completely different: We watch the sun set in front of us and rise behind us. The horizon is completely different.

When we are reborn, through an unexplained spiritual phenomenon or through a decision on our part to change our lives, we change directions. The ship is the same — we are the same person — but we are going in a completely different direction. Spiritually, this means that instead of mapping our own course, we are allowing the Lord to be our guide.

We can make this decision to orient ourselves toward the Lord. But what if we're feeling sad, discouraged, hopeless? It's especially important then because we really yearn for and need a guide. Does the Lord want us now, when we are feeling bad? He always wants us. What a wonderful time to ask for a rebirth into a life in union with Christ.

After all, being reborn means living a new *kind* of life, putting away the old and taking on the new and wonderful and learning to make Christ the center, the horizon, and the guide, all at once.

DAY 23

. . . your benefit is sanctification as you tend toward eternal life.

Romans 6:22

I read somewhere that if your heaven does not begin on earth it never will. What can this mean to you and me when we are discouraged? Surely, this is not heaven — this combination of thoughts and feelings that bring us down, that frighten us, that cause us to wonder why we are here at all.

The message is that we ought to expect happiness in this life, that we can look forward to joy. We are not bad; we are not unworthy; we are not mistakes. We are here on this earth because of the love of a Creator who wanted us because of, not in spite of, our humanness.

Our eternal life begins with our human life here on earth. God made us not only to be happy with him in the next world but also to be happy with him in this world. Centering our lives on Christ, trying to live a life that is directed toward getting closer to the Lord, is the way to heavenly happiness and the secret to happiness in this life.

How can we reconcile our need for happiness with the suffering we experience? Remember:

> We do not deserve suffering just because this is our earthly life.
> We shouldn't think that suffering is inevitable.

> We should do all in our power to deal with and overcome our suffering — whether it takes the form of physical pain, emotional distress, or spiritual trial.

When you feel discouraged, it is not that God wants you to be distressed. He wants you to be happy. You can be happy. Don't think of happiness as a package, sealed and tied with a string, a package that is inaccessible to you. There are steps you can take to find your own happiness.

First, you can convince yourself that you ought to be happy. Why? Because you are a person whom God loves and whom he wants to be happy, as each of us wants happiness for those we love. You desire happiness, of course.

Second, you can actively seek happiness by confronting the issues that seem to be standing in the way of your happiness — difficulties with health or personality or relationships that are painful.

Third, you can begin right now, today, to do those things that bring you happiness. Start with little things that bring you a bit of joy — telephoning a friend, going out to lunch, taking a long bath, reading a book, playing the piano, lying on a hammock, baking a loaf of bread, looking at a photo album. Obviously, different things bring happiness to each of us. You know what makes you happy.

If your state of depression makes you feel that nothing will make you happy, start by doing something that made you happy in the past. Though you may not reach the same degree of happiness you had in the past, the effort will bring a certain amount of satisfaction; and that is a good beginning.

DAY 24

The willingness to give should accord with one's means, not go beyond them.

2 Corinthians 8:12

Forget yourself by thinking of others — fine advice, no matter how you're feeling. But when you're feeling bad, it's especially healthy and helpful to do a little something for someone else so that your concentration is not on what you are suffering — what you lack — but on what you can give.

You ask, "What can I possibly give? I feel so bad, no one wants my help. I'll just make everyone else miserable. Besides, there is so little I can do."

When we're discouraged, we tend to think in the negative about what we *can't* give instead of what we can give, of what we *can't* do instead of what we can do. We're overwhelmed by our problems, and forget our real abilities.

But stop your brooding for a moment and try to be a little more objective. Admit this: You have gifts. You do! If you find this hard to believe, ask your best friend what he or she considers your best gifts. Then sit down and ask yourself:

What do I like about myself?
What do other people like about me?
What do I consider my most beautiful quality?
Do I have talents that I can develop? What are they?

Let's not compare ourselves with other people: "I'm not so great. I'm not a good cook like she is." "I don't have a good education." "I can't tell a story like he can." "I wish I could sew like that." "I wish I could draw that well."

Too often we fall into the trap of assuming that we have to be able to do all kinds of things exceptionally well in order to be able to give. The truth is, we only need to do a few things or even one thing well. We can lack certain abilities completely and have only average ability in other areas. I always think of a famous singer I've long admired. The man sings beautifully. He doesn't have to do anything else well. He doesn't write music or play an instrument. In fact, it is possible that, except for his singing ability, he is quite ordinary. But that one gift, his voice, is the key to his bringing happiness to millions of people. And the most important thing is not just that he *has* this gift but that he shares his gift.

If you are eager to give, and if you do give, whatever your gift is it will bring something to others. You don't have to reach millions of people; you need reach only one person to make it all worthwhile. Whatever your circumstances — as a homemaker who deals with a small number of people or as a person in the media or politics who deals with thousands — it is the gift and the giving which are important.

You are not judged on the basis of what you cannot do. Continue to give from what you have; that's what makes you wonderful. Don't apologize for what you do not have; that is for those to share who have it.

DAY 25

God chose those whom the world considers absurd to shame the wise; he singled out the weak of this world to shame the strong.

1 Corinthians 1:27

You may be impressed with people who seem to "have it made." But do you identify with the person who has reached the top of the mountain, the "star," the person who seems to have no problems? Probably not. The reason is that it is very hard to feel close to people who have no troubles. We can learn little from them, especially if we feel we are at the other end of the stick — struggling, barely making it.

When the above Scripture passage talks about the wise and the strong, it speaks of those who use their knowledge and power to get ahead at the expense of others. Real wisdom and true power put to the service of others are good and admirable. The message is that it's the very people whom the world laughs at who really have the answers, not those whom the world holds in high esteem. There are some uneducated laborers who know far more of the things that really count than some professors in prestigious universities. And there are professors who are truly wise but who use their gifts quietly to educate young people.

Learning about the most unlikely to succeed who succeeded — people who achieved sainthood or meaningful success in the world — makes us feel hopeful because they show us what is possible for each of us. We needn't be famous or rich in order to be really wise and to achieve something.

We are intimidated by people who wield great power and hurt others in the process; there is something diabolic about it. In amassing wealth and concentrating political control, men seek to compete with the Almighty.

If we feel foolish, we are in good company. Many of those who did great work for the Lord were made to feel absurd. They met rejection, humiliation, pain. But through their experience they grew in the Lord. When you and I feel pain and sadness, we experience a need for the Lord and have a wonderful opportunity to grow close to the Lord.

Sometimes people who are in pain, who must see a physician or be hospitalized for surgery, feel embarrassed or foolish. People who suffer emotional difficulties such as depression may feel embarrassed because they face the need to seek professional help. People undergoing spiritual trials may feel terribly alone and foolish. If you feel this way, try to see that you are not really foolish; there is no reason for embarrassment. God will help you to grow through your neediness and possibly to go on to help others grow.

In the end, it is the people who are considered weak who are actually strong because they teach quietly, without a lot of fanfare, without the need for lots of personal attention. They use the present moment and the inspirations that come unexpectedly to teach the real lessons of life.

DAY 26

Continue, therefore, to live in Christ Jesus the Lord, in the spirit in which you received him. Be rooted in him and built up in him, growing ever stronger in faith, as you were taught, and overflowing with gratitude.

Colossians 2:6-7

We need to remind ourselves of who we are. Christ is with us all the time. We grow spiritually through an awareness of this. "Placing yourself in the presence of God" is an expression that describes what we do to heighten this awareness. We say, in effect, "Lord, I know that you are with me." Knowing this, we become more confident because we feel that we have the Lord as our companion throughout life.

We can do anything with Christ's help. While we may know our limitations only too well, we can be sure that whatever strength we lack will be supplied by Christ. We can multiply the power of our gifts by dedicating their use to his service. We can grow as people, stronger, more courageous, more loving by consciously joining forces with him.

You know when you plant a tulip bulb in the fall that by springtime the plant will bloom. But you have to prepare the soil; you have to set the bulb properly. You do not see what takes place over the winter months; you simply trust that something is going on because that is the way bulbs are supposed to act. In the early spring, sure enough, perhaps on a day when April snow is melting, you see shoots piercing the soil. Sometimes things go wrong, but not often. As long as the bulb takes root, you are reasonably assured of a healthy plant.

It's like that with us. We have to be deeply rooted in the Lord in order to be spiritually healthy and to grow. If we are rooted in the proper environment, we flourish. But unlike the plant, we have control over whether we stay rooted in the Lord. He has planted us firmly, but we have to choose to stay with him. We must keep our roots deep in him who is our support.

In times of trouble, in a storm, it's amazing how strong a plant can be if the roots are firm. In stormy times in our lives we need this type of strength. Our roots in the Lord give us that strength.

Practically speaking, choosing to stay rooted in the Lord means:

> reminding ourselves that the Lord is with us;
> accepting the spiritual help that the Lord offers —
>   prayer, the Scriptures;
> getting into the habit of thanking the Lord for his help;
> training ourselves to ask for help whenever we need it,
>   no matter how great or how small our needs are;
> weathering the storms by hanging on: asking for and
>   getting support;
> reminding the Lord that he has promised to help.

When we feel discouraged, it's a good time to reinforce the deep conviction that we can rely on the Lord. We may not *feel* very strong, but we know that we have a source of help. The truth is that, whatever our feelings, the Lord is our help and our strength, our basic support in all days, stormy or sweet.

DAY 27

Make it a point of honor to remain at peace and attend to your own affairs. Work with your hands as we directed you to do, so that you will give good example to outsiders and want for nothing.

1 Thessalonians 4:11

Living our everyday lives is sometimes the most difficult challenge of all. We have to deal with the same people, the same family members with their same faults; to work at the same job, with the same supervisors; to put up with the same problems of health, money, schooling; to accept the same "me."

Usually, people are not burdened with trials that are truly foreign to their environment or way of life; the kinds of problems they have to deal with are the problems people have dealt with since time began. In a sense, the problems are not new; but the way each person takes on his or her burden, the way each person lives out his journey to the Lord, is unique. Millions of people have had family problems; how you and I handle ours is unique because we are unique. Millions have had to deal with chronic pain; the stories of how they coped are varied. Many have suffered emotional difficulties; how they handled them has depended on many distinct factors.

Because we are human, we may wish to escape our humdrum existence, our everyday burdens. Some people do try to forget what is wrong by blocking out what they feel. Some coping mechanisms are healthy enough; but others are not — leading to depression, illness, or dependence on drugs or alcohol.

No matter where we go, we will have to adjust to the fact that, except for a few moments here and there, life is not exciting. We work hard and, at times, have a special feeling of accomplishment, but the feeling is temporary. Even in our spiritual lives we may have occasional times of great devotion, when our feelings are just wonderful, but this does not last. We could not handle ecstasy on a regular basis.

The scientists who win the Nobel Prize are the center of attention for a few weeks and, then, return to their laboratories to take up their day-to-day routine existence. Their day of glory falls into place among many, many ordinary days. College students have a special day of recognition, Graduation Day, after working hard at their studies. Mothers and fathers are remembered at special times, but then go back to "the old grind." We all get used to this.

Ideally, we get to the point where we are not waiting around for the fireworks, those moments of sheer joy. We try to find joy and fulfillment in our everyday lives. When we feel discouraged, it becomes more difficult; but our daily routine helps us muddle through. While it may be tempting to abandon all projects and just do nothing, it's much healthier to try to do what you usually do — to get your work done and to find a little joy in that.

DAY 28

Rejoice always, never cease praying, render constant thanks; such is God's will for you in Christ Jesus.
1 Thessalonians 5:16-18

It's hard to pray when we feel bad. We become depressed, tend to think less of ourselves, and feel ignored or slighted by others. So we don't feel up to bothering God either. We feel embarrassed to pray.

When we do pray at such times, we feel that we need answers to a lot of questions. But the plain truth is that often God does not "answer" as we expect him to; his answers are sometimes in the form of other questions. Or he does not answer immediately or solely in terms of what *we* think we need. Many people in great pain have cried out, "Let me die!" God does not take them unless it is time for them to die. Their emotions seek a solution which is not at all in their best interest. We are usually anxious to have an answer NOW, even though our problems are quite complicated and have been with us for years.

When we feel bad we may not pray because we wonder whether it will do any good. Here again, negative thinking gets in our way. Though we have prayed in the past and God has helped us, our feelings block the memory of those times.

We may question our ability to pray. "How can I pray? I can't even think straight." Then we shouldn't think too much. Just tell the Lord that we feel so bad we can't think straight, but we need him very much.

We don't need to be contemplatives whose lives are dedicated to prayer to pray properly. The "prayer of a simple man" is fine: "Lord, I need you. Please help me as you always have. I love you."

This is the time to be like children. Have you ever received a note from a young child who is just learning to print? dEEr MOM i luV yOu LISA. Not perfect spelling, not perfect printing, but very special because of the love with which it was written, the love which it conveys, and the relationship which it reaffirms.

When we feel discouraged, it's OK to share the insecurity, the dependence, the childlikeness with the Lord. We can go back and be the needy child, the little person who is overwhelmed with the world that seems so big. It's OK to be afraid or uncertain, to cry, to laugh, to wonder, to question, to leave questions unanswered.

When we feel bad, let's try to think in a positive way about prayer. We can help ourselves by holding on to our beliefs:

I can pray.
The Lord wants to hear from me, no matter how I feel.
I can tell the Lord what is wrong without embarrassment.
I don't need to say much; I can listen.
I can just be there with the Lord, and I am praying.

DAY 29

. . . I want to sing with my spirit and with my mind as well.
1 Corinthians 14:15

Singing is a form of prayer. That's evident in the hymns that we sing in church, addressed to God.

Singing with the spirit is not just the vocalizing of a clear lilting soprano or a strong baritone voice. It is not simply the on-key, in-time rendition of music and lyrics. When your heart sings it has a music that is more than sound and vibration: it is alive and fills you with vitality and joy. Your whole being is in tune with life.

When we feel discouraged, we may not feel like singing. Ordinary music may make our depression worse, because our emotions are so in conflict with the feelings to which it gives expression. The music of the soul, of the spirit, may not seem to be ours to play.

But let us look forward hopefully to a time not far off when we will be singing for joy, when our whole being will sing a new song of love. This should not be the dream of the desperate but something we are consciously working on and approaching. Little by little, through faith, we should be moving toward a sense of worth that will make life start playing its song for us.

What is meant by our "spirit"? It is our inner life, our heart, our feelings, our hopes, our love. It is the inner self that is aching to come out. It is that best self that we sometimes reveal in moments of self-acceptance, in moments of exhaustion after trial, in the calm after a long battle with a problem.

We can also sing with our "mind." We have talked about the need to change our thinking, to get away from the negative and to replace it with the constructive. Too often we continue to bear the scars of damage done to our self-image long ago. We judged ourselves harshly and listened to the false evidence of others but now refuse to rehear the case.

Our emotions are not an accurate gauge of the state of things. Sometimes we feel guilty when we have done nothing wrong. We feel useless though we are very worthwhile. Though possessed of a strong, quiet faith in the Lord, we still don't feel religious. With many reasons for hope, we feel helpless. We feel empty though full of and surrounded by riches.

When we feel bad, we ought to try to figure out why. What kind of negative thinking has caused the bad feelings? What kinds of messages from the past are we listening to? Are we being too hard on ourselves? Are we expecting too much from ourselves and not enough of the Lord?

We will be able to sing with our minds — that is, to think constructively and positively — if we get rid of the old ugly thought patterns and gradually replace them with new ones that are beautiful and constructive. We can start today with a few kind thoughts — about ourselves!

DAY 30

Be on your guard, stand firm in the faith, and act like men. In a word, be strong. Do everything with love.
1 Corinthians 16:13-14

When we send a little son or daughter off to school, there is a pep talk. "Chin up. Study hard. Work hard. Remember what we taught you." It's a way of saying "Farewell and good luck," and an opportunity to say a few words which might be remembered when the door closes behind him or her.

If we had to find a little pep talk for you, after these thirty days together, the advice from First Corinthians would certainly fill the need.

Be on your guard. Take charge; take control of what is happening. Do not allow sadness to get the best of you. Fight it; work to replace it. If things get bad, find help. If you reach a point of desperation, WAIT.

Stand firm in the faith. Our faith is tested not when everything is going for us but when we have reason to question. When we're feeling low, everything seems difficult. We may be unwilling to put out the effort that believing demands. But if we can just "hang in there," even when the Lord does not seem to be listening, the time will most assuredly come when we realize that he is listening and always has been listening.

Be brave. "Whistle a happy tune," they say. How can you be brave when you are shivering with fright? when you are almost paralyzed by fear? You can if you remember one fact: You are not alone. There is Someone there to guide you through the dark tunnel of your sadness, Someone who will not let go. You may not recognize him until the struggle is over and you can say, "I don't know how, but I got through it."

Be strong. Try to act as if you felt strong. As we have said, it is hard to be strong when you feel so vulnerable, but you can begin to be stronger by simply acting — by taking the initiative. Act as you would if you were strong, and you will be strong. Fooling yourself? No. By achieving something, however small, you begin to build confidence in yourself and to really have inner strength.

Do everything with love. You don't feel very loving. You feel sad; you feel angry; you feel depressed. But though you may not feel like the hugging, caring person you want to be, you can act out of love, act in such a way that you show that you do love and care for others. Action is a matter of motivation, not feeling. And when love comes from you, it will most likely return to you. And that will certainly help.

Repeat the words from Scripture or words like them. Let them become yours. And believe them. Begin by wanting to believe them and, before you know it, you will.

GOD LOVES YOU!